PRAIRIE DOG COLORING BOOK

CRYSTAL
COLORING BOOKS

ISBN: 9781673677133

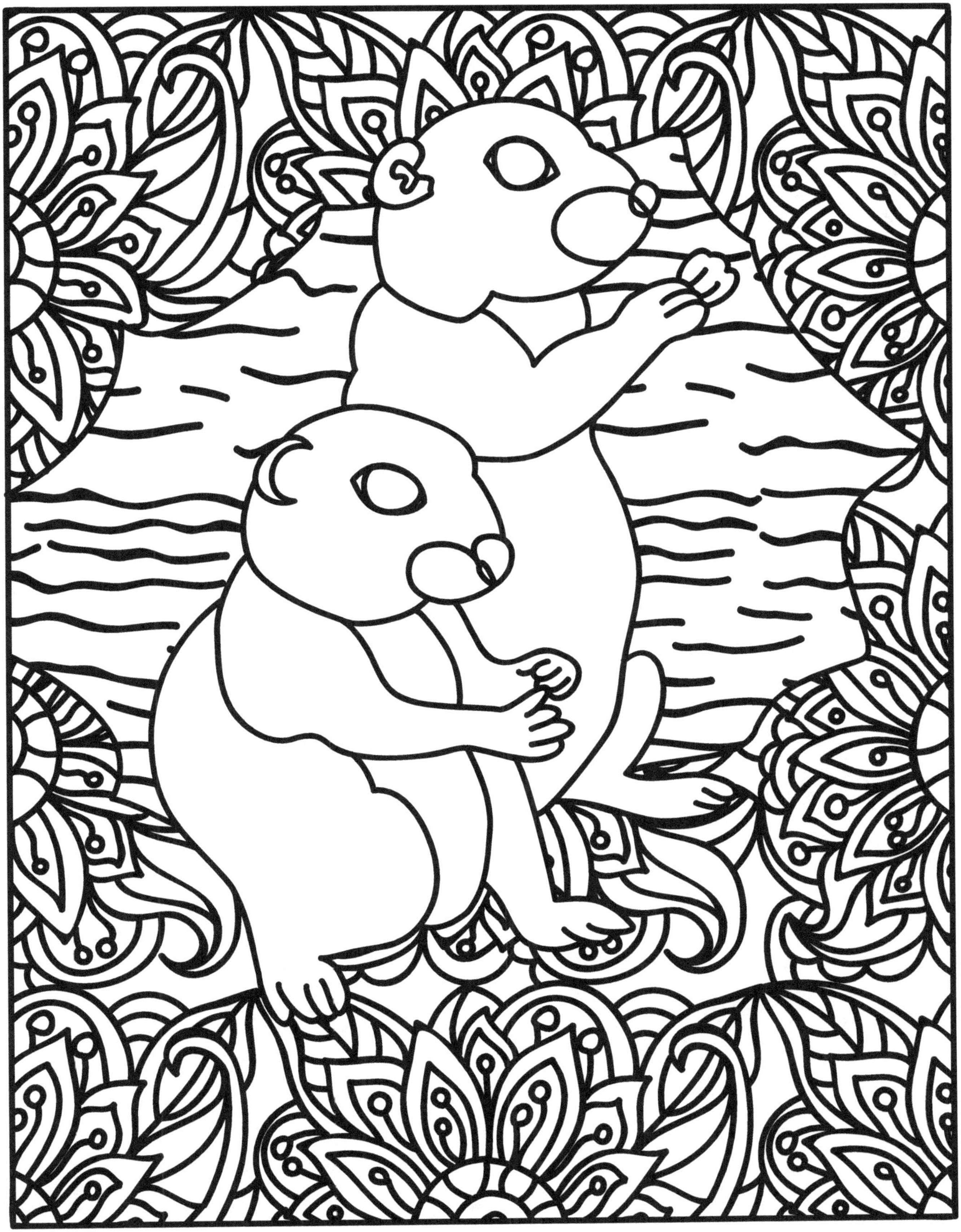

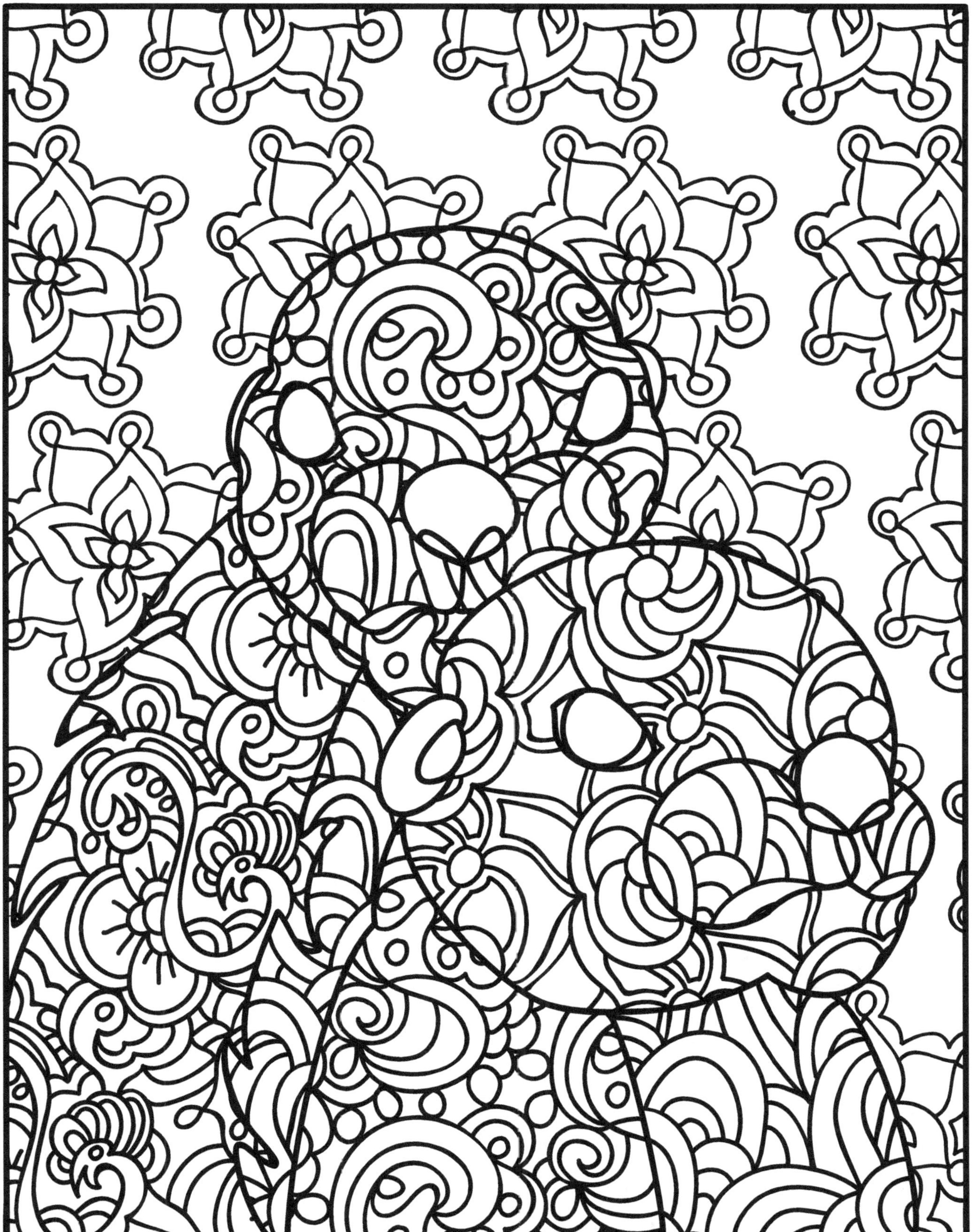

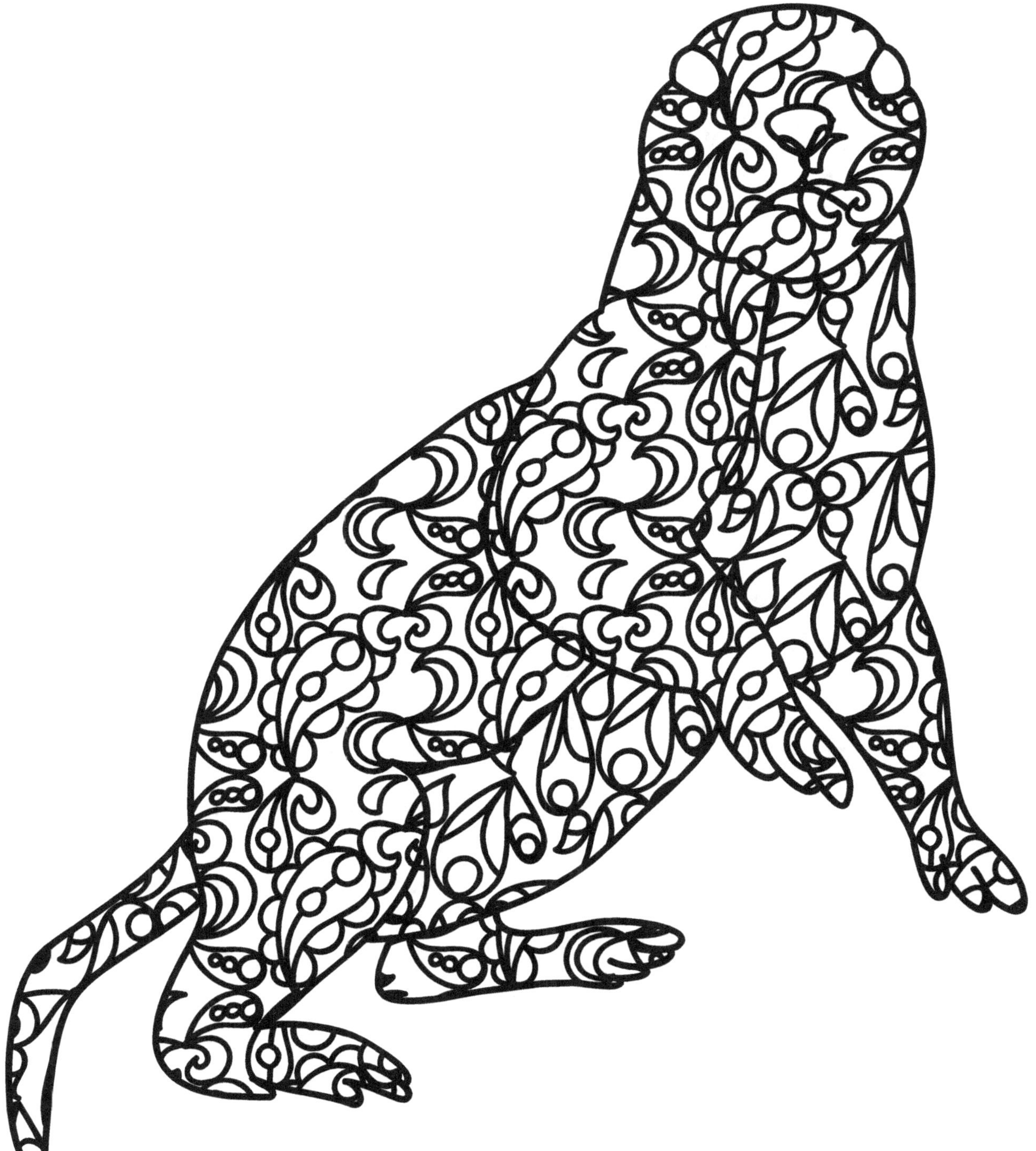

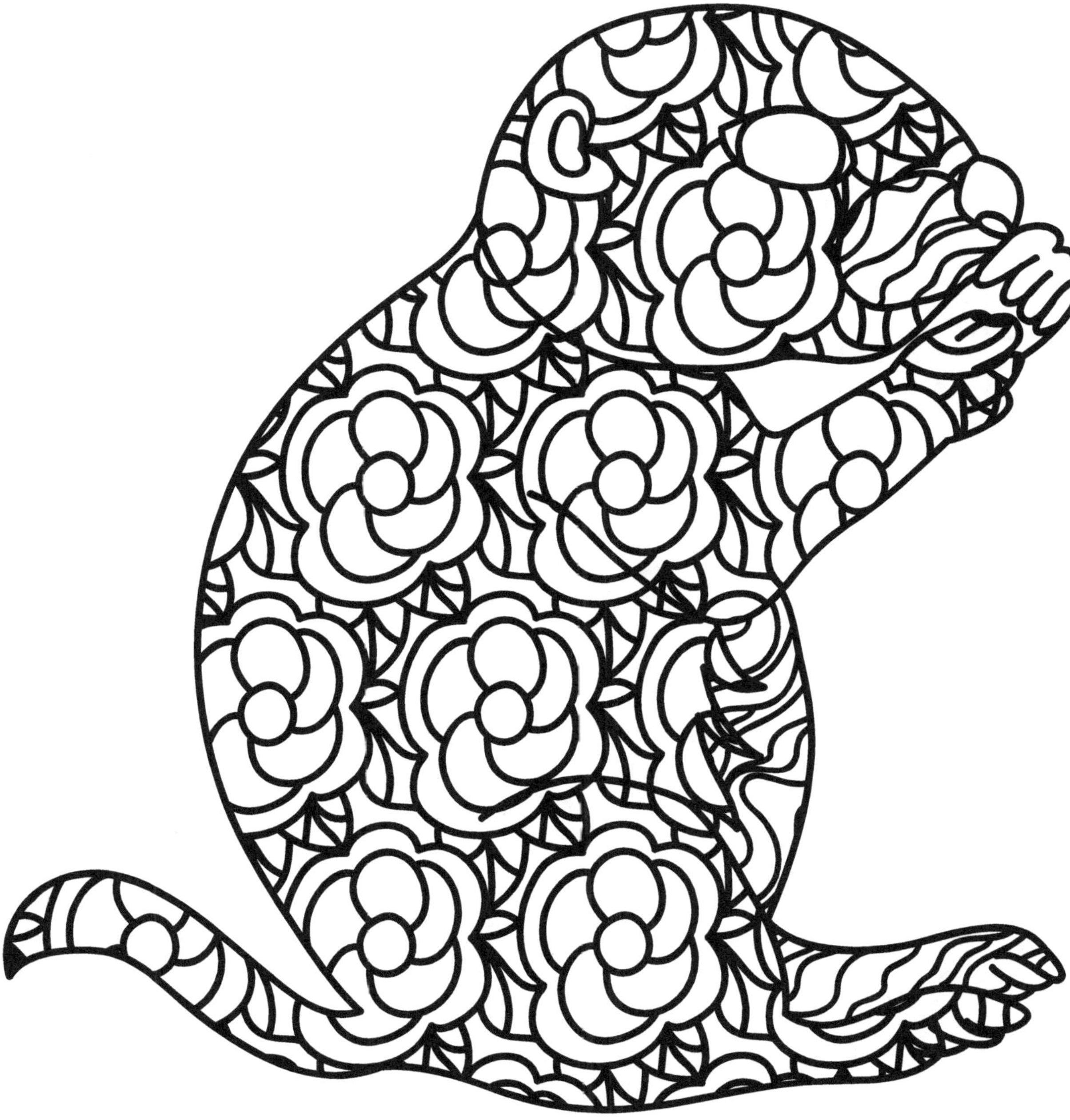

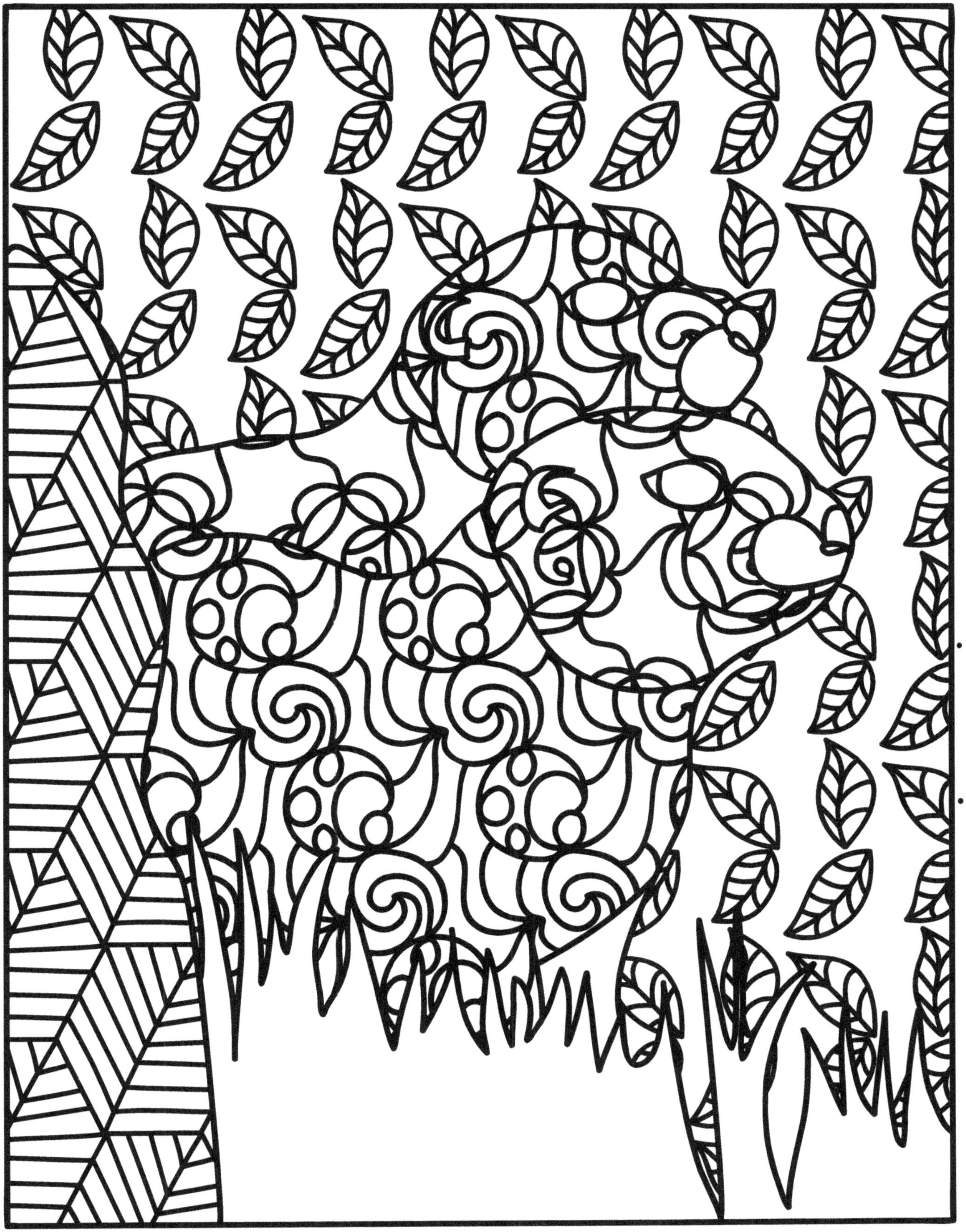

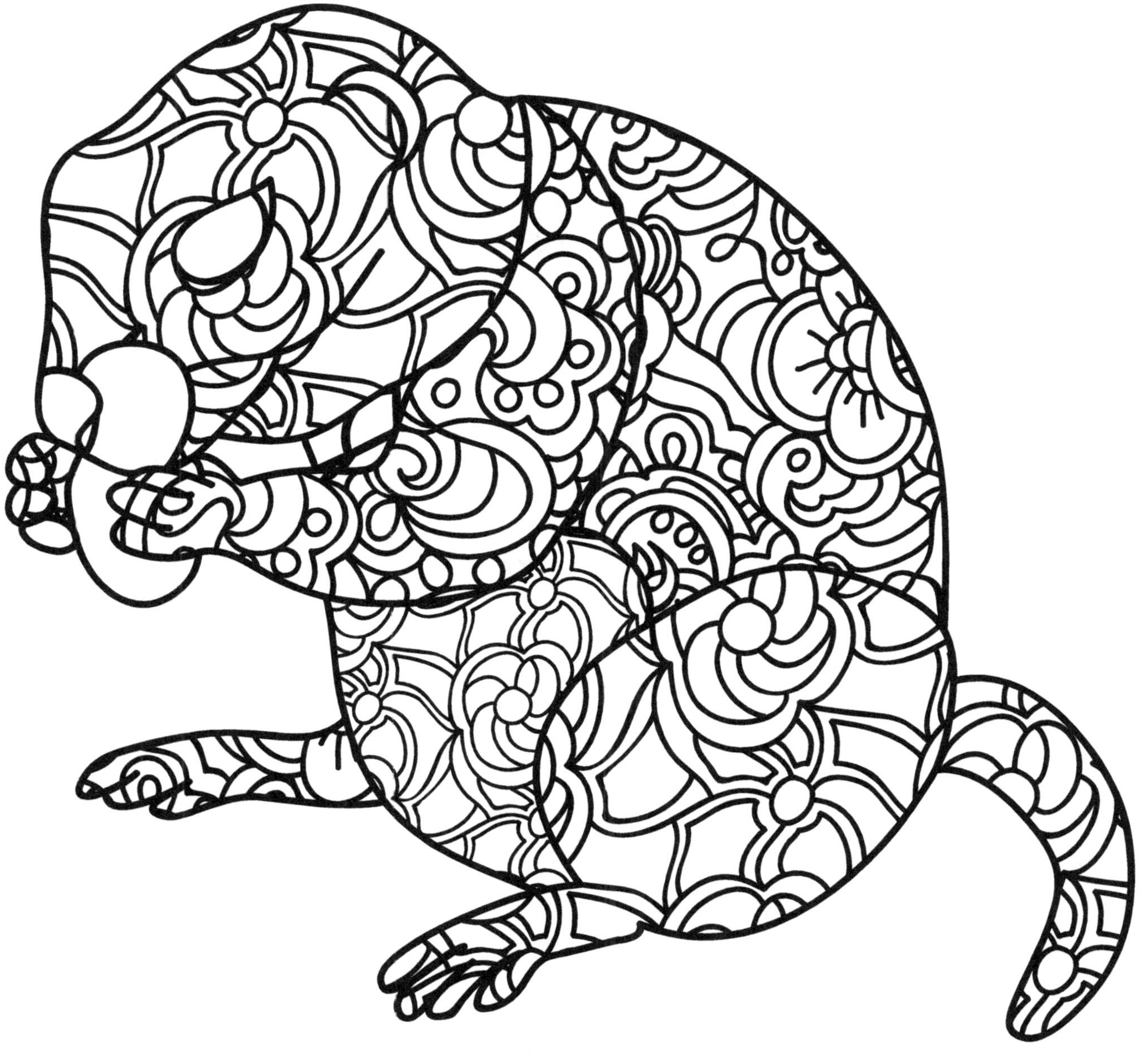

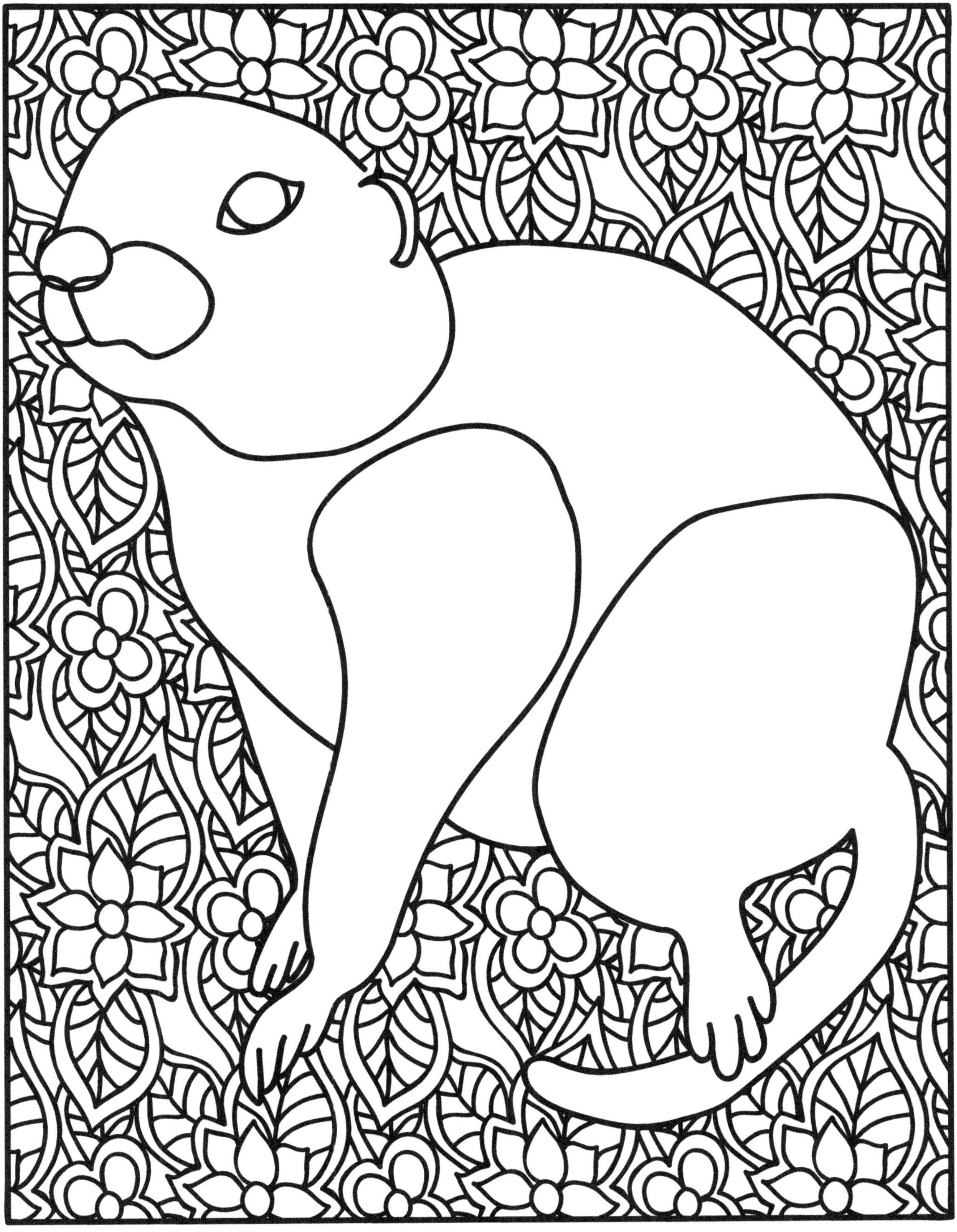

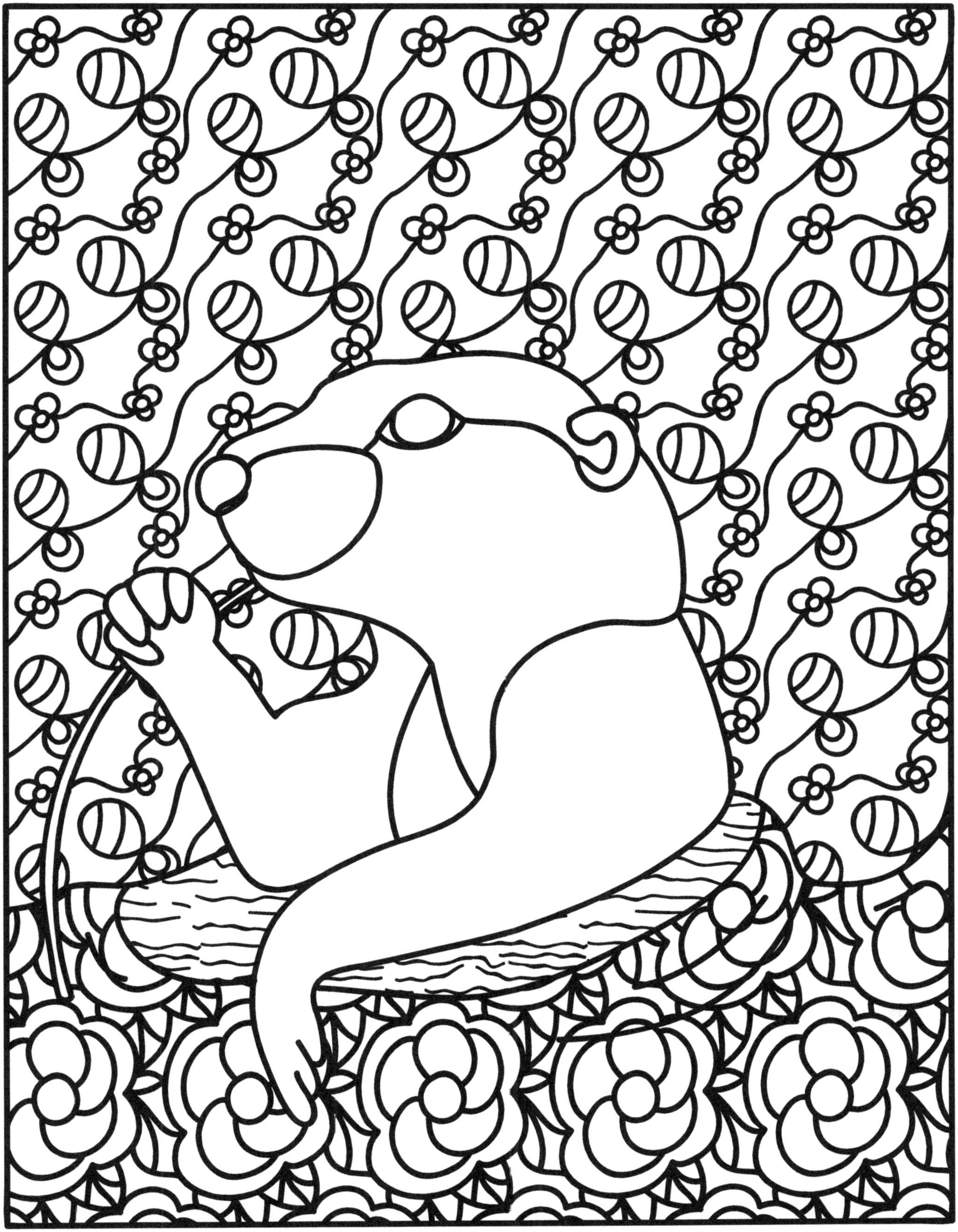

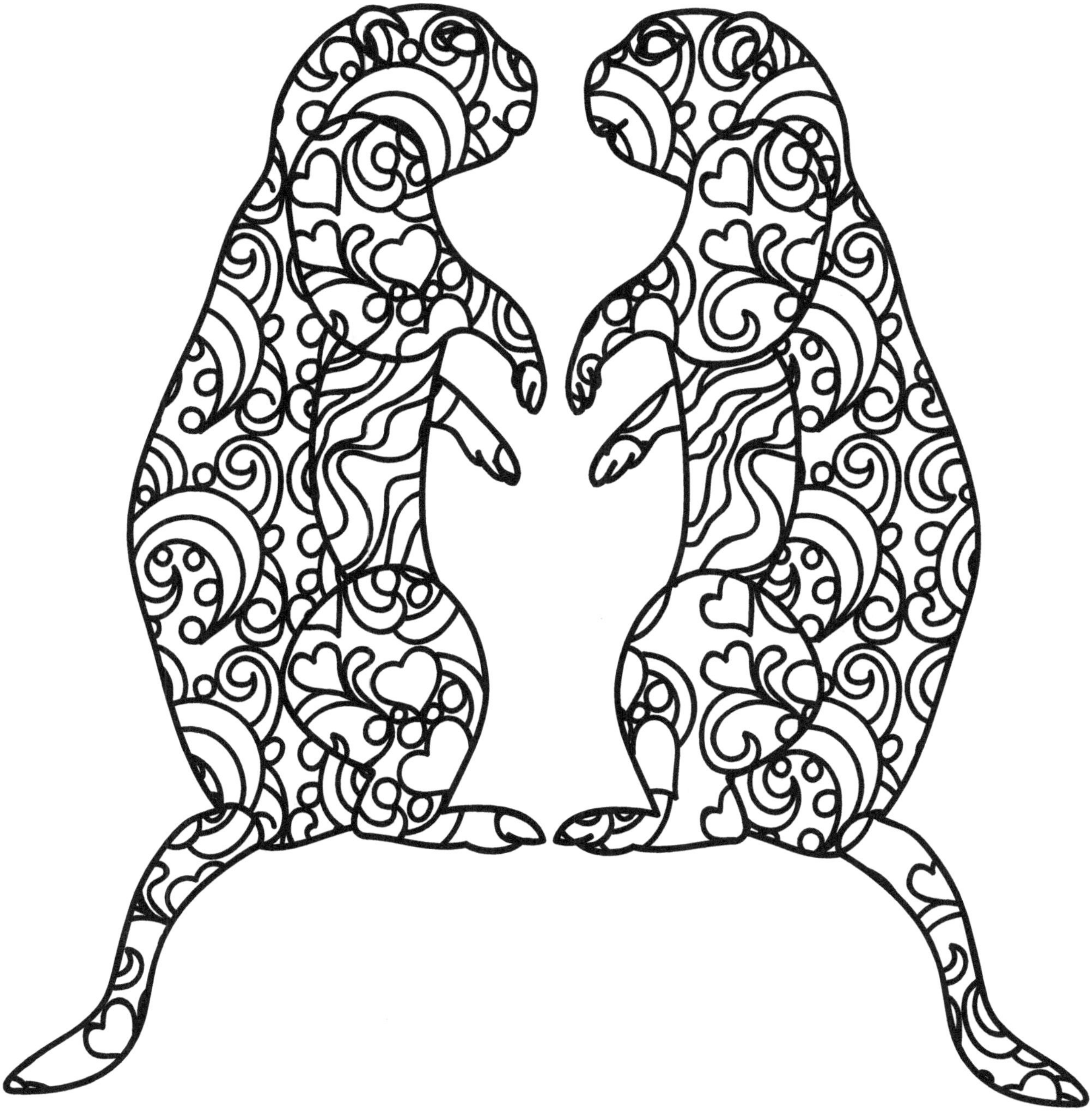

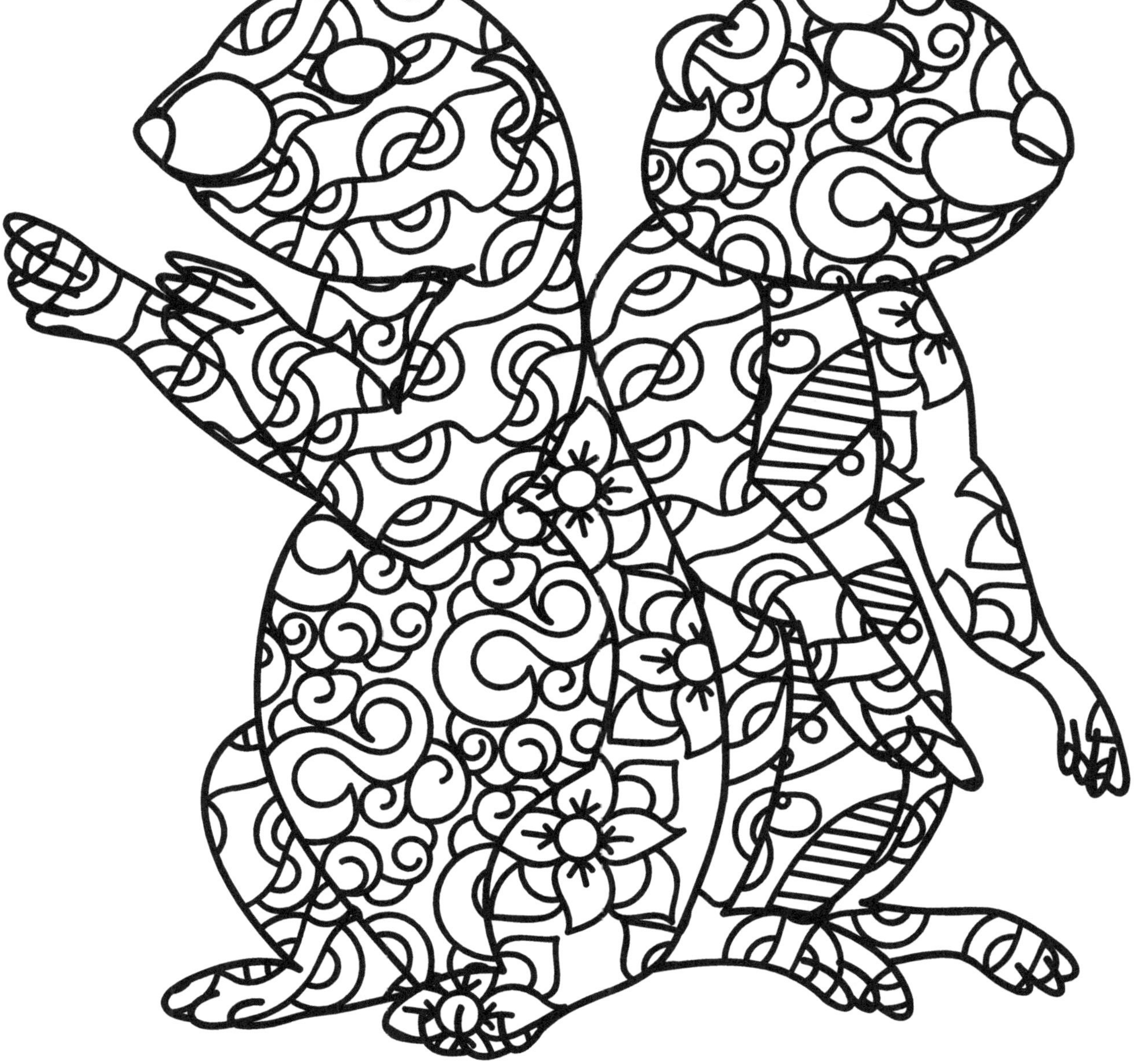

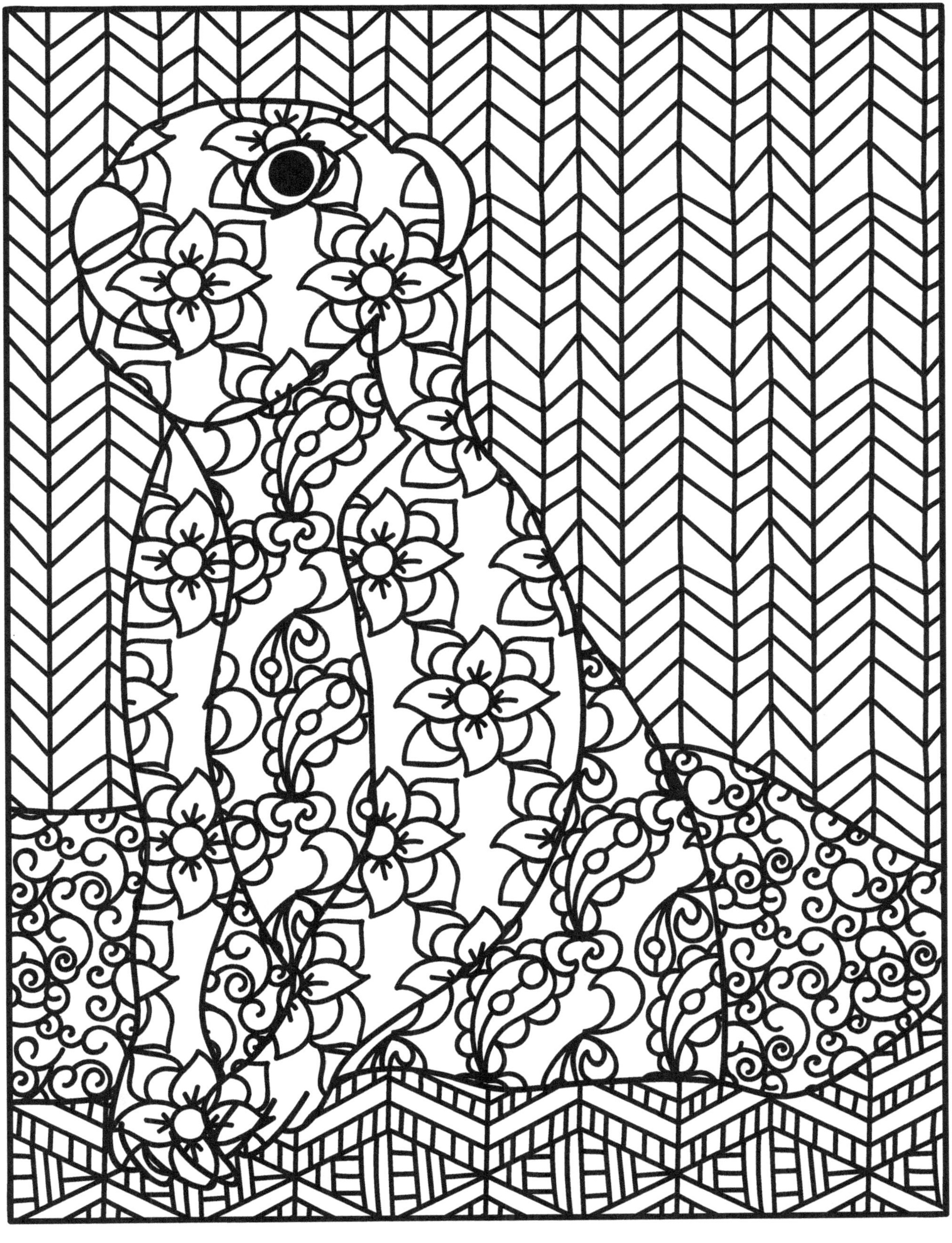

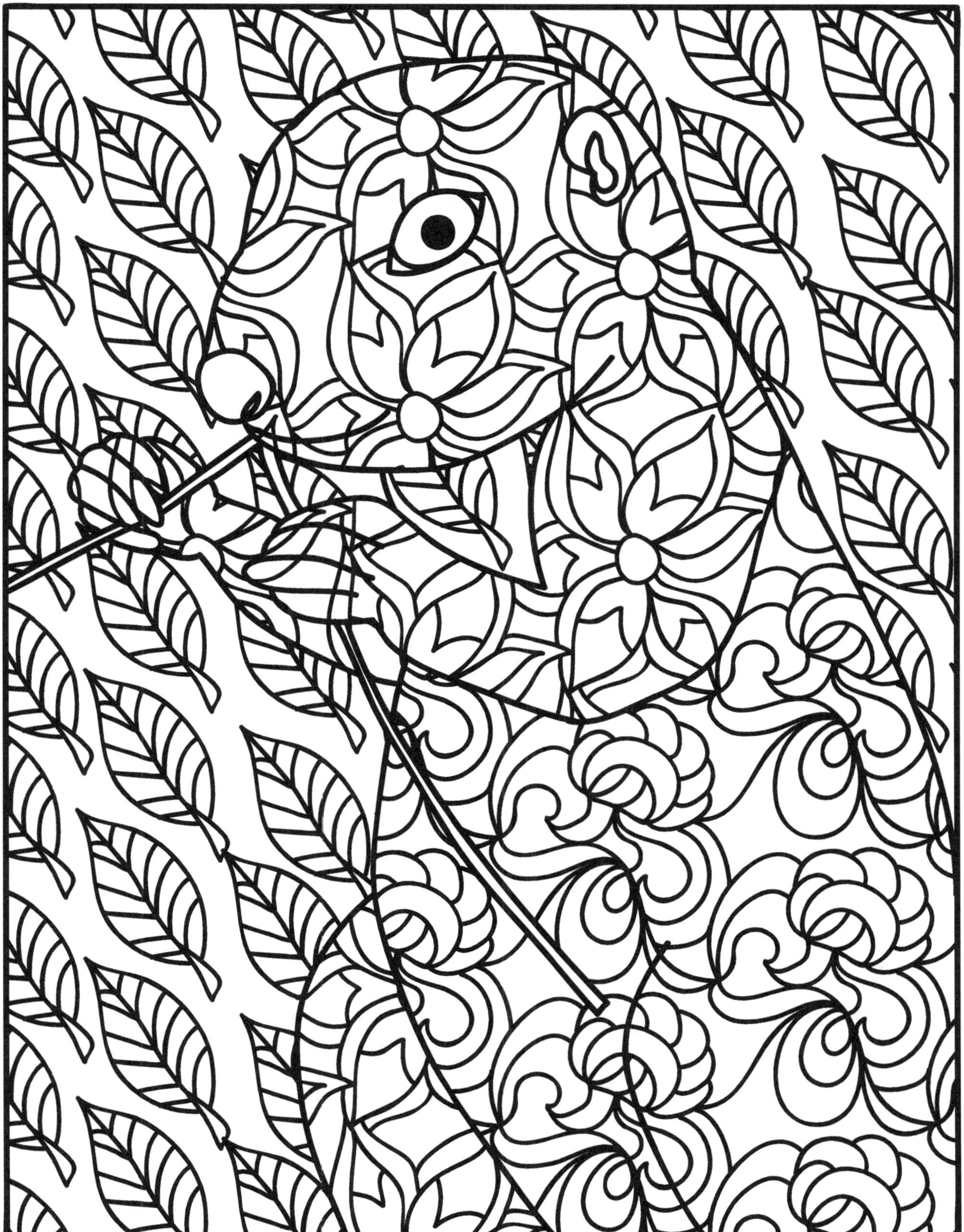

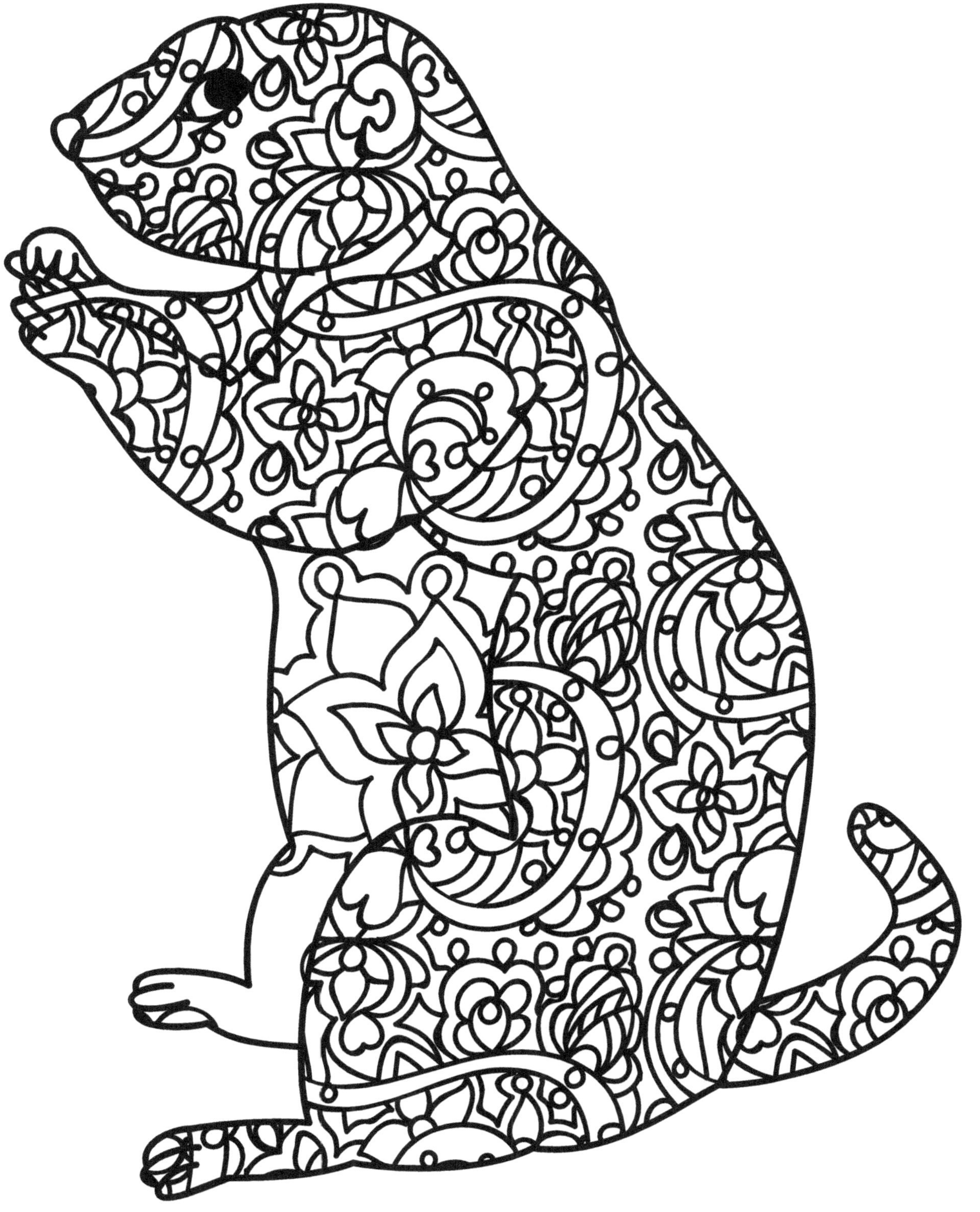

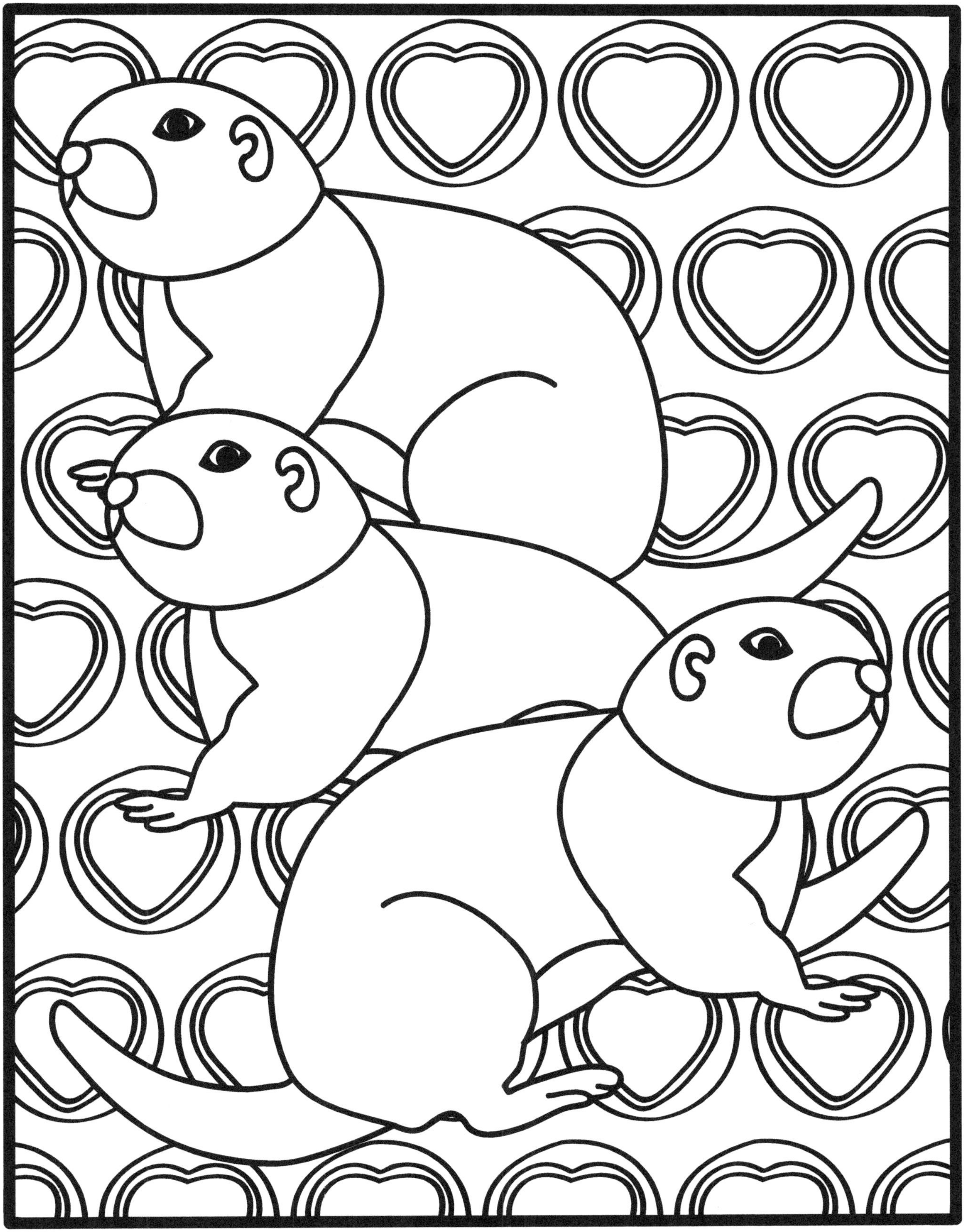

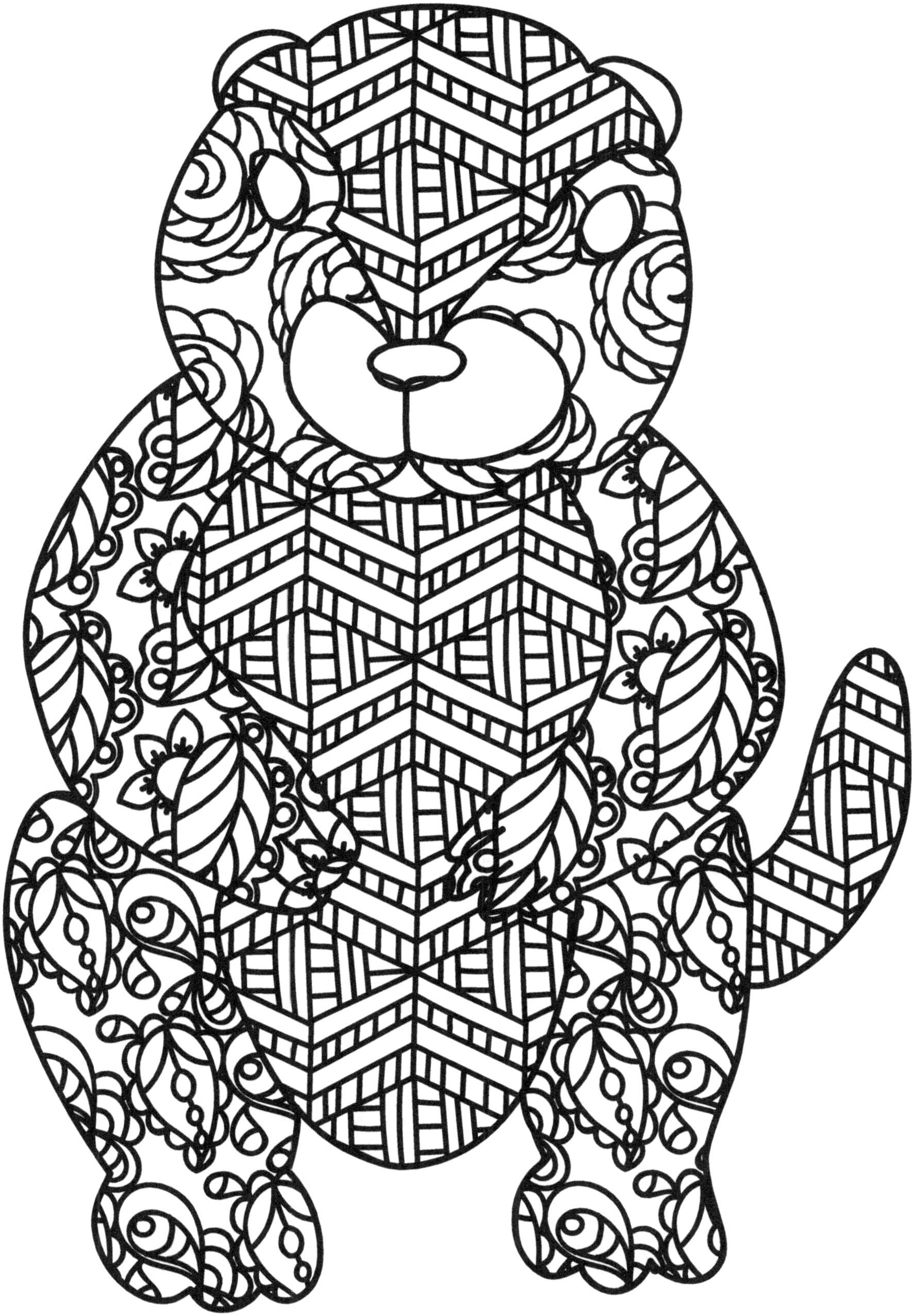

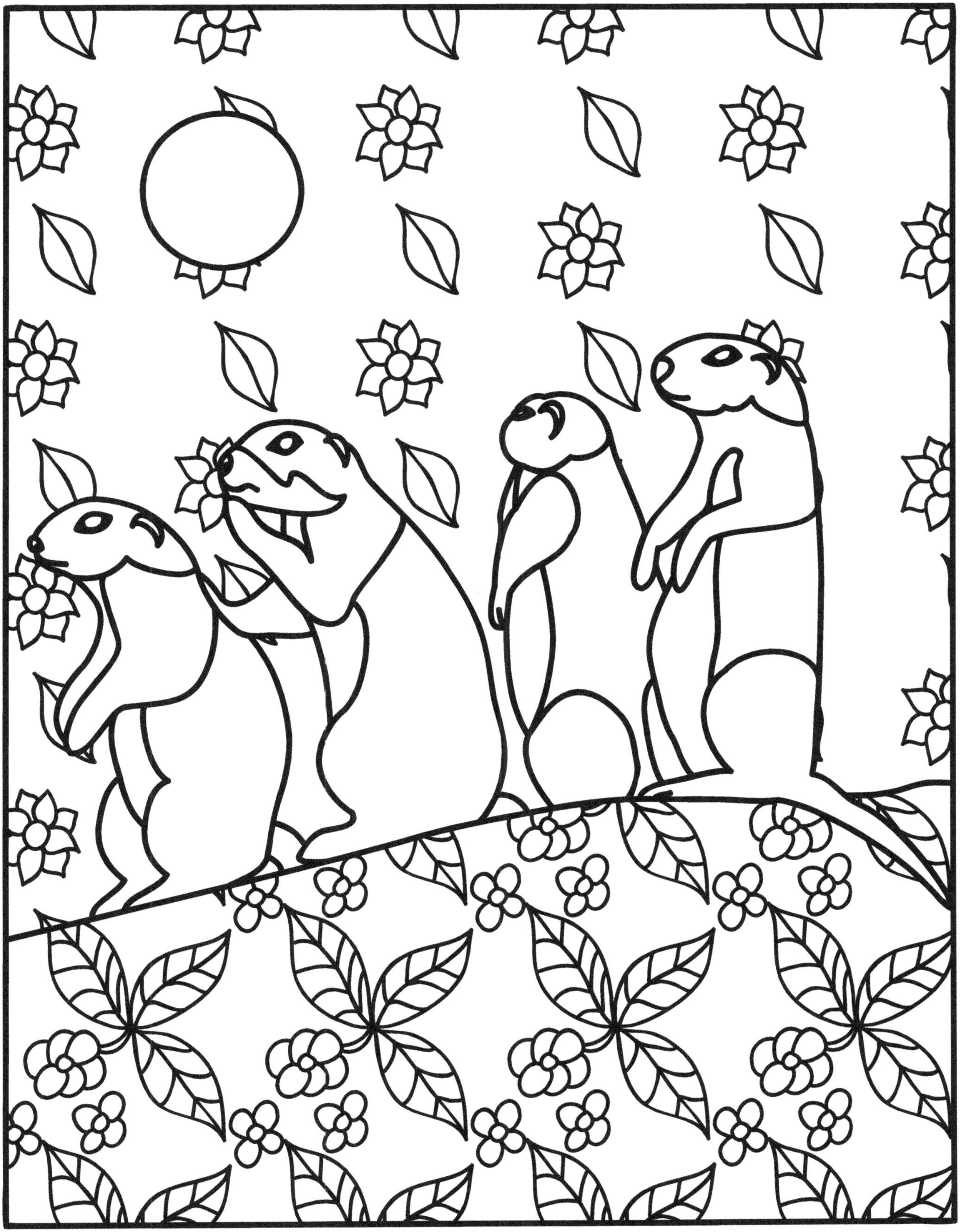

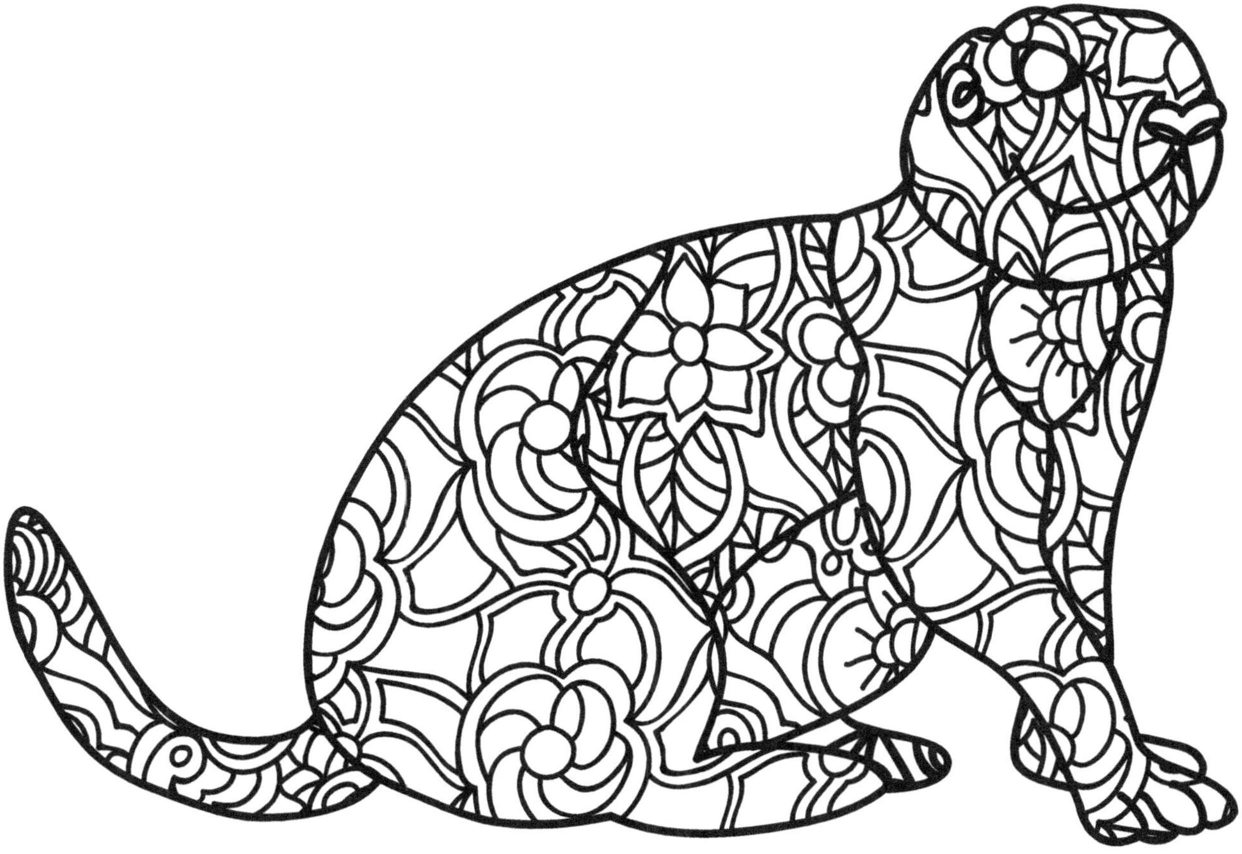

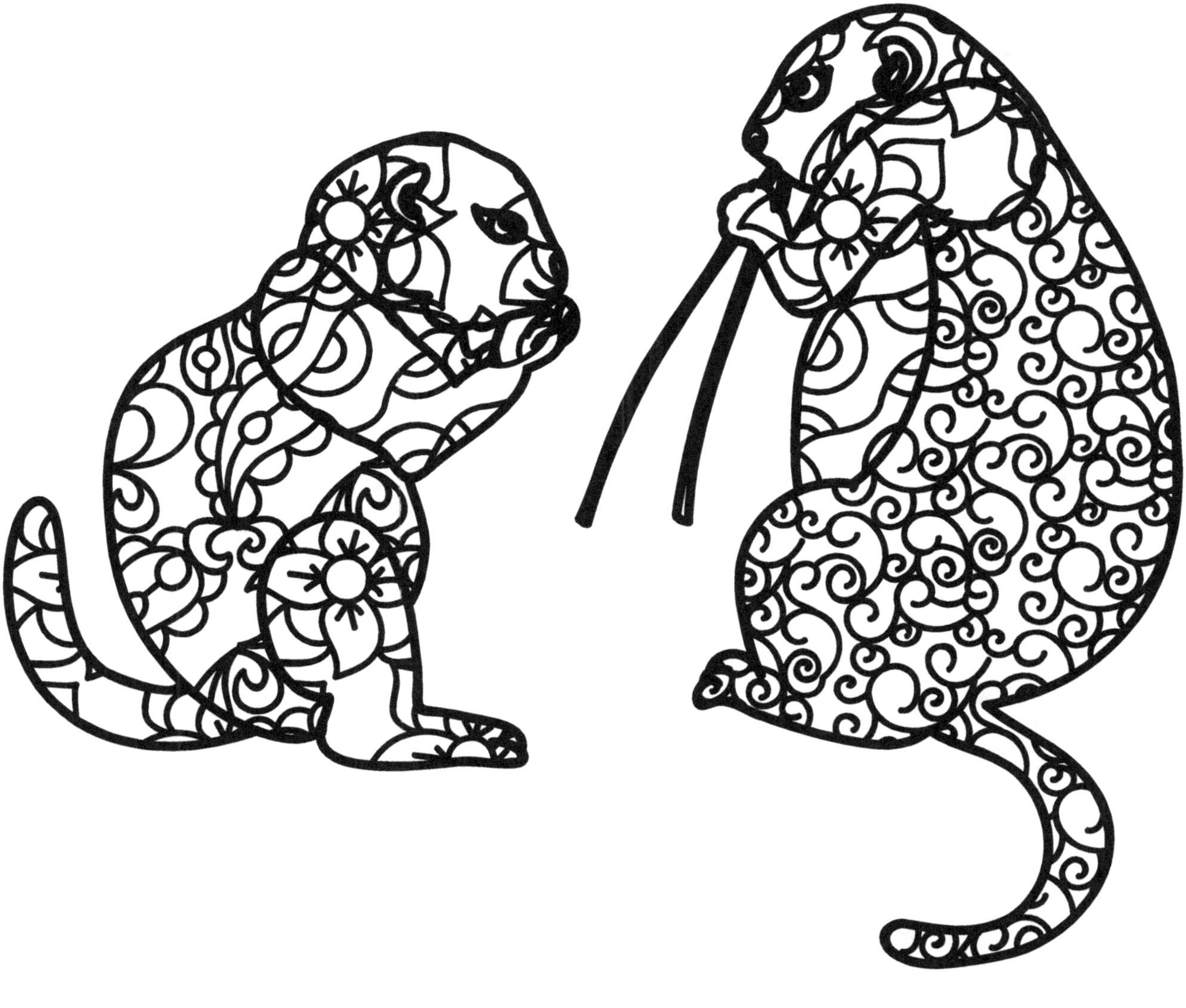

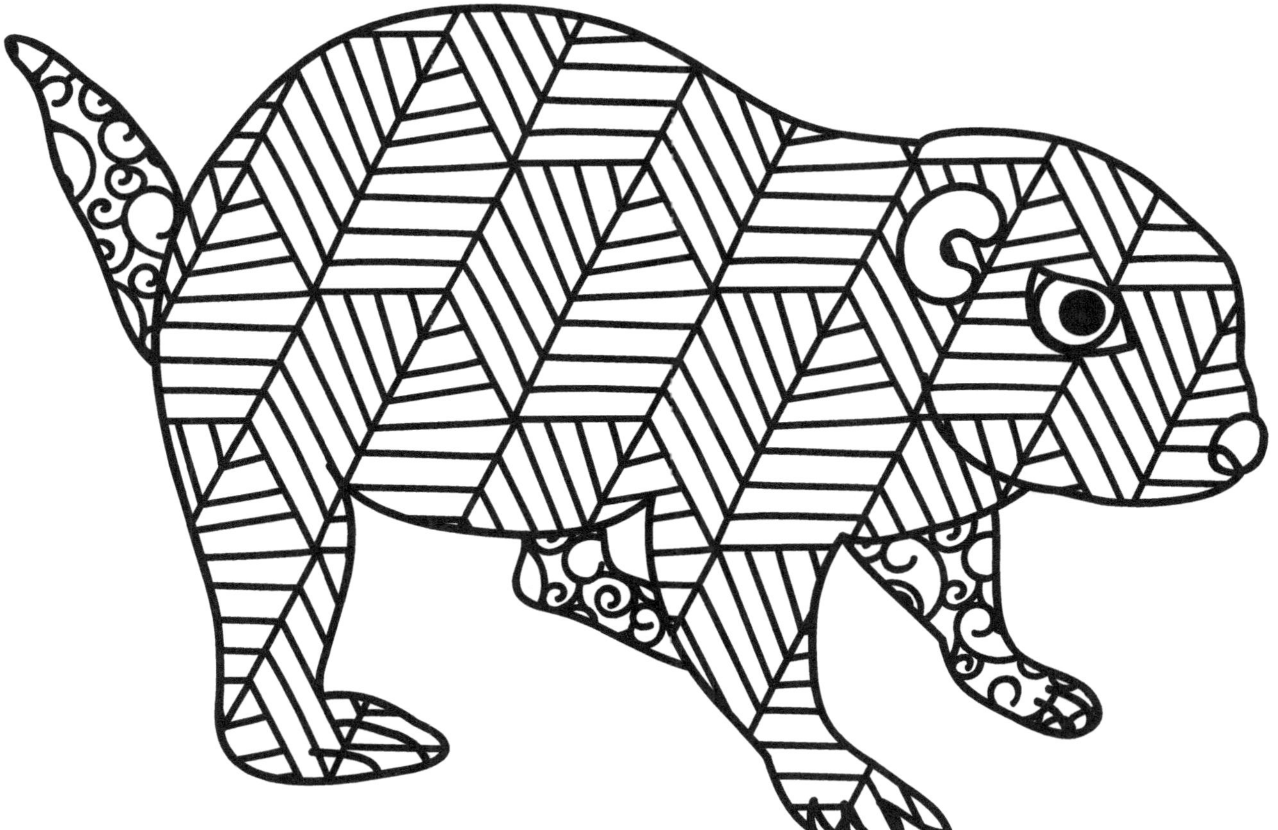

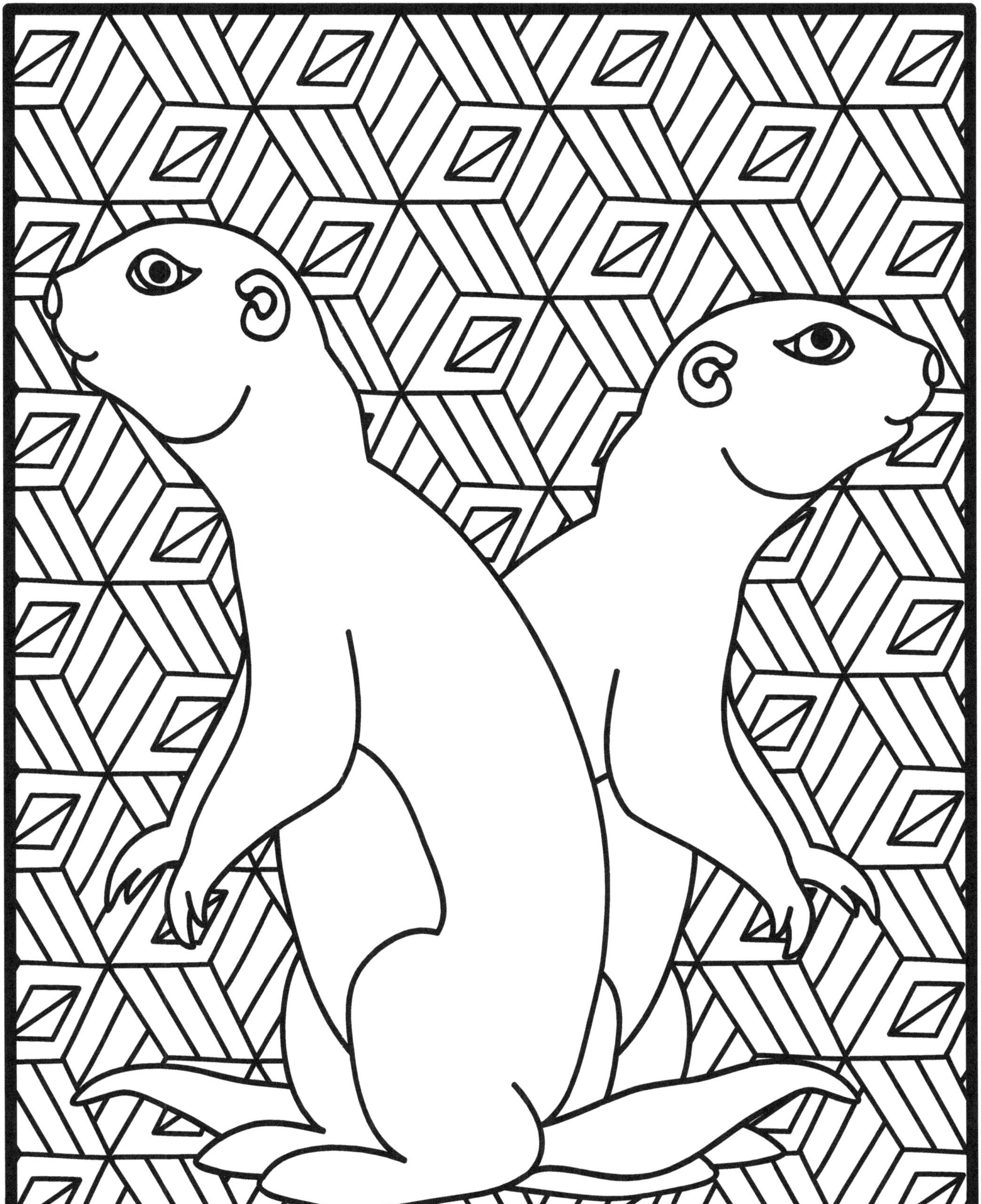

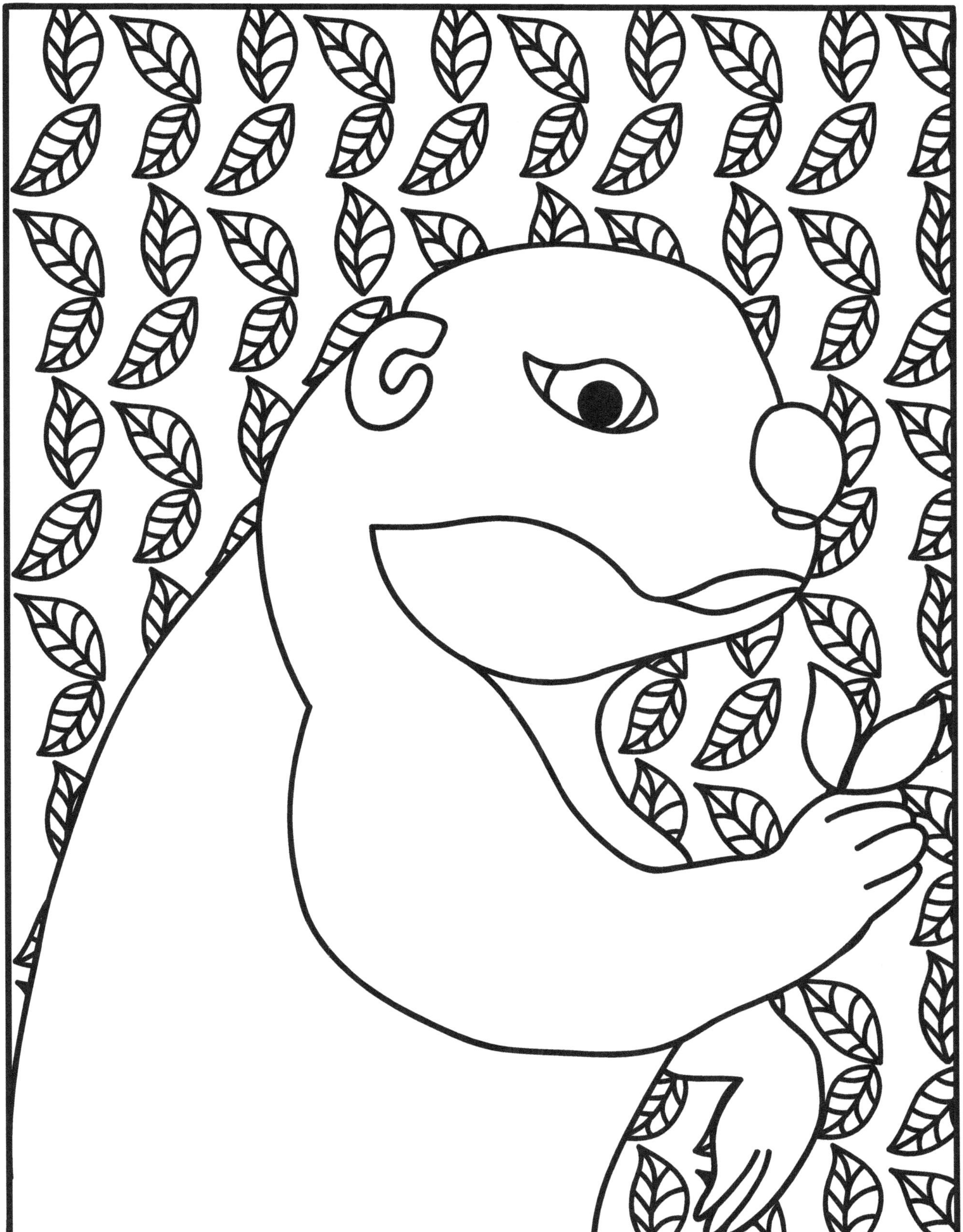

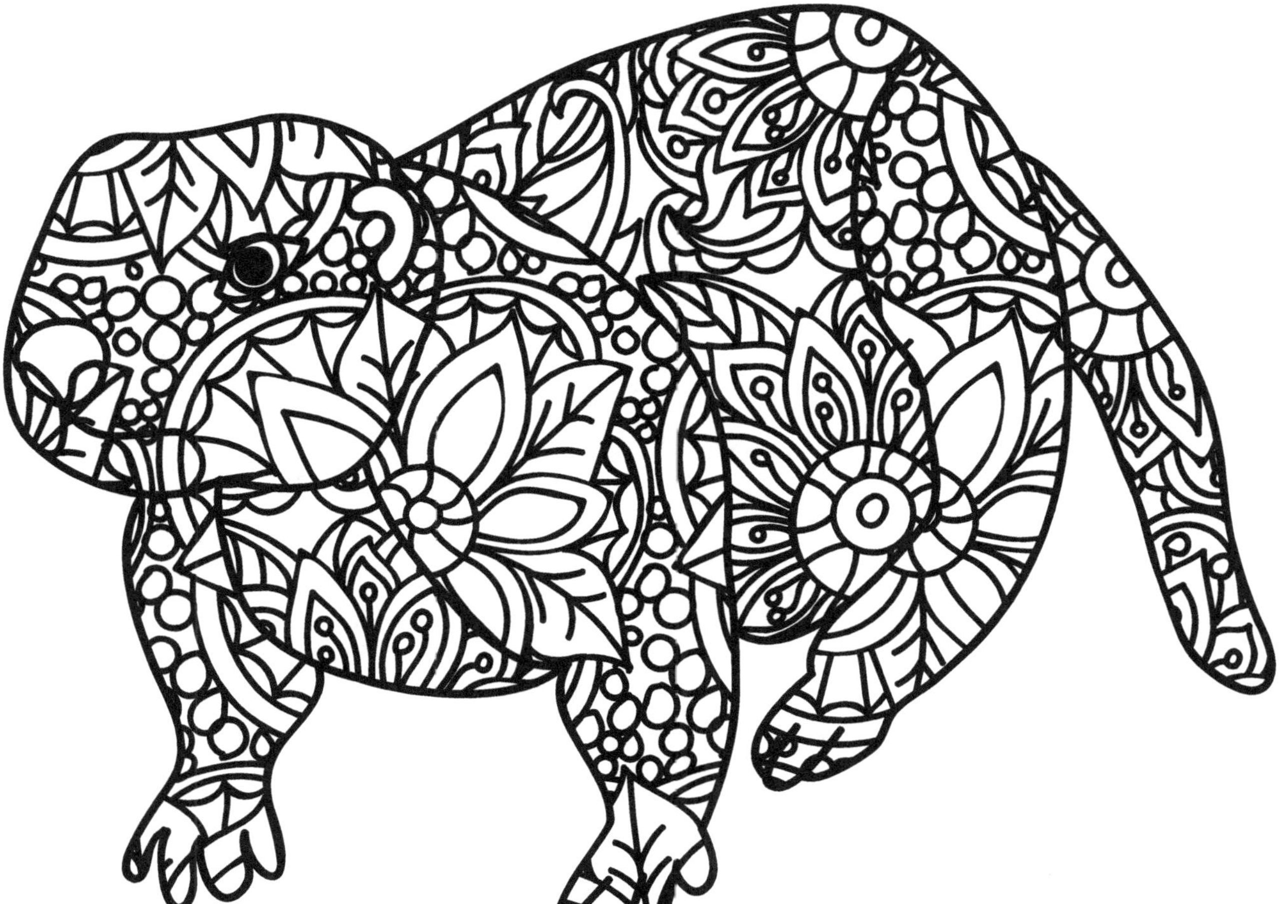

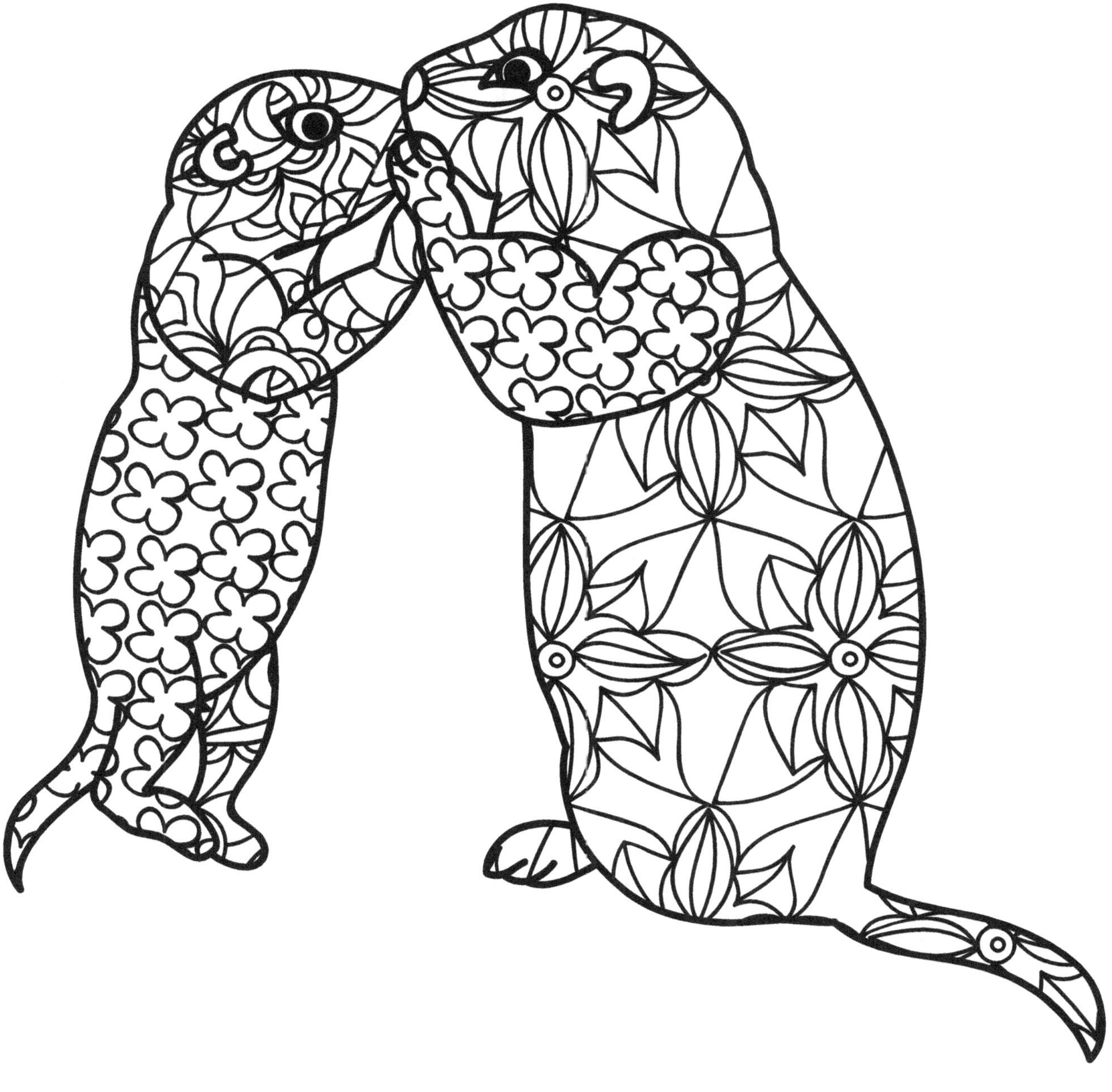

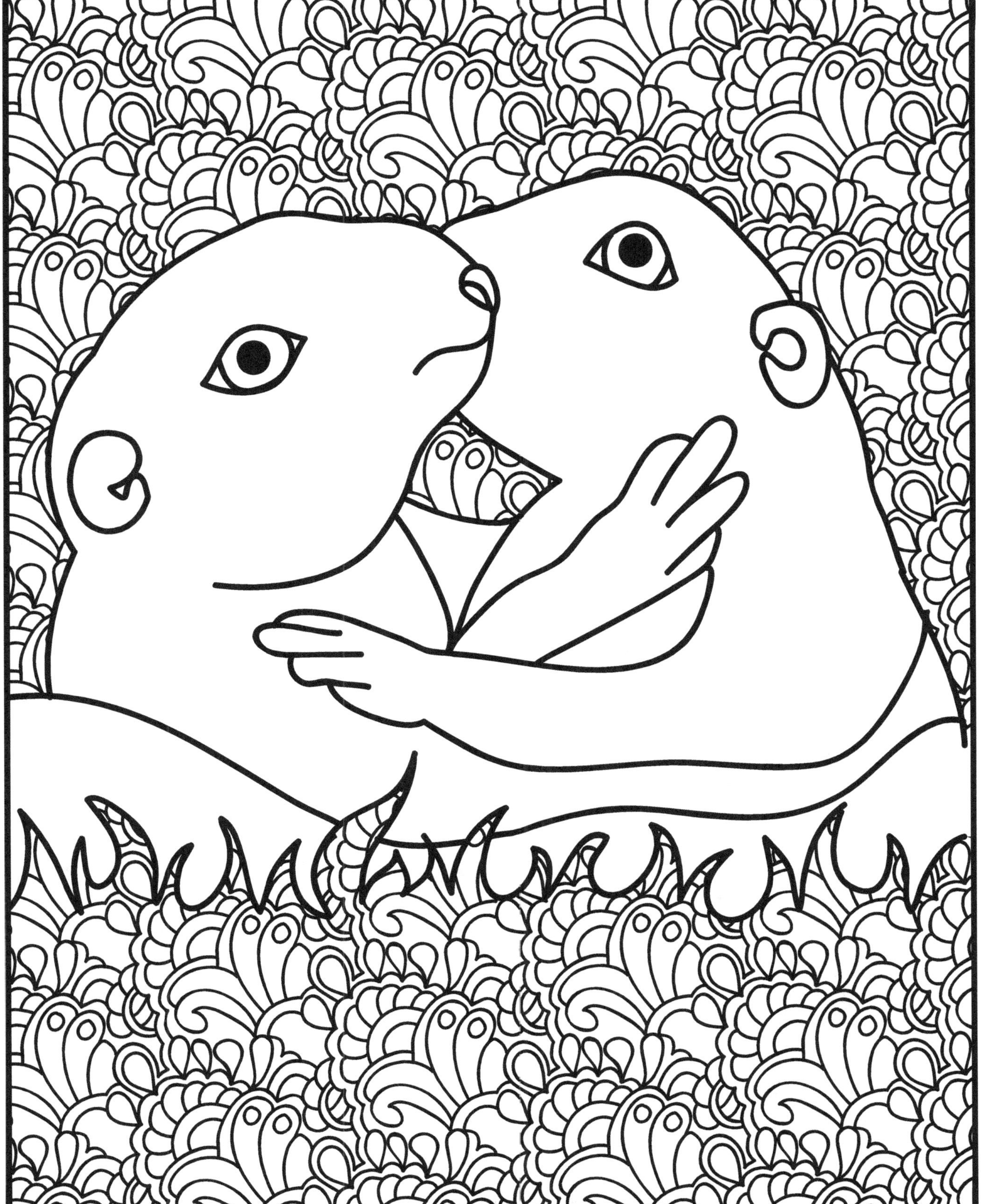

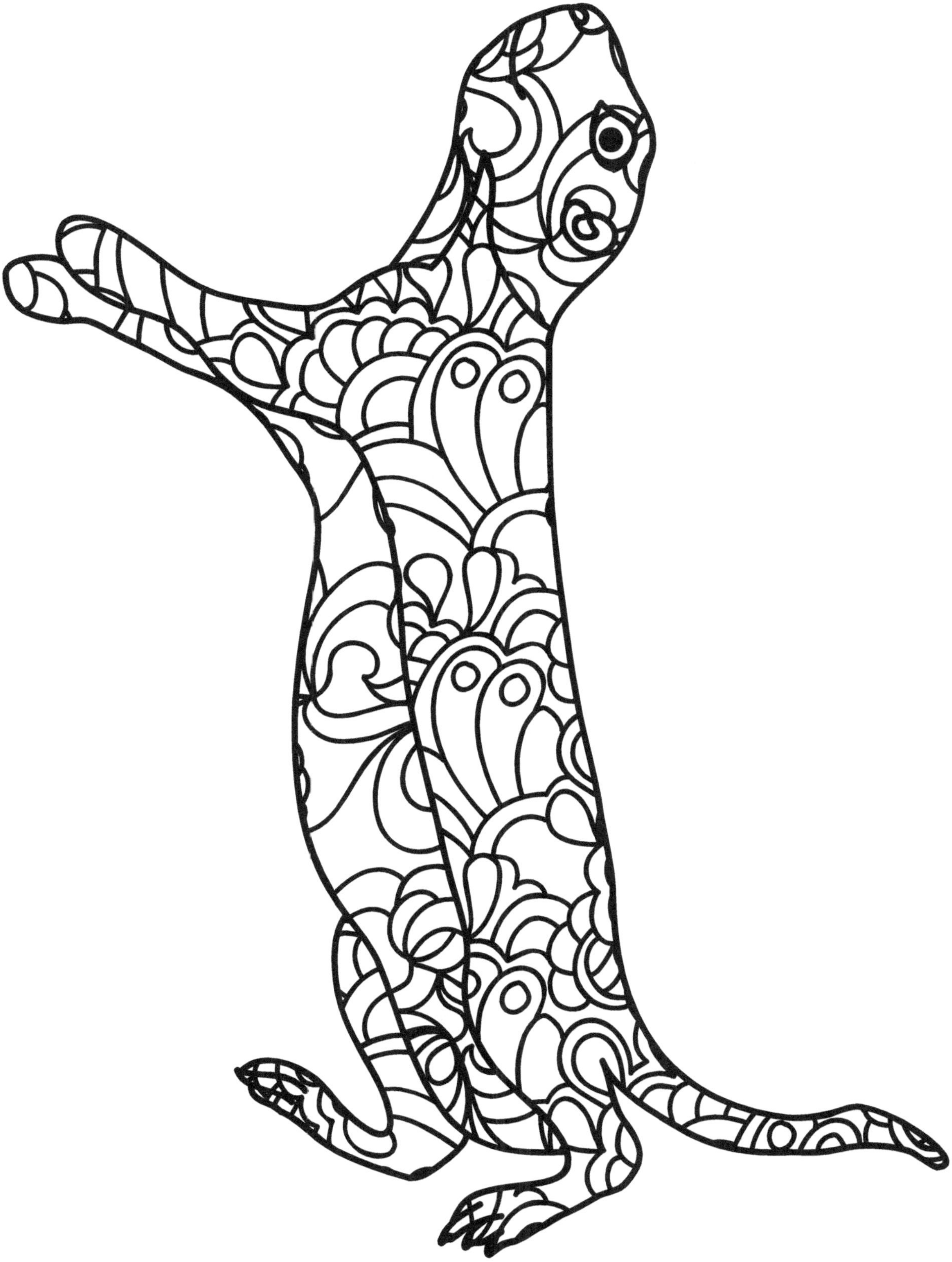

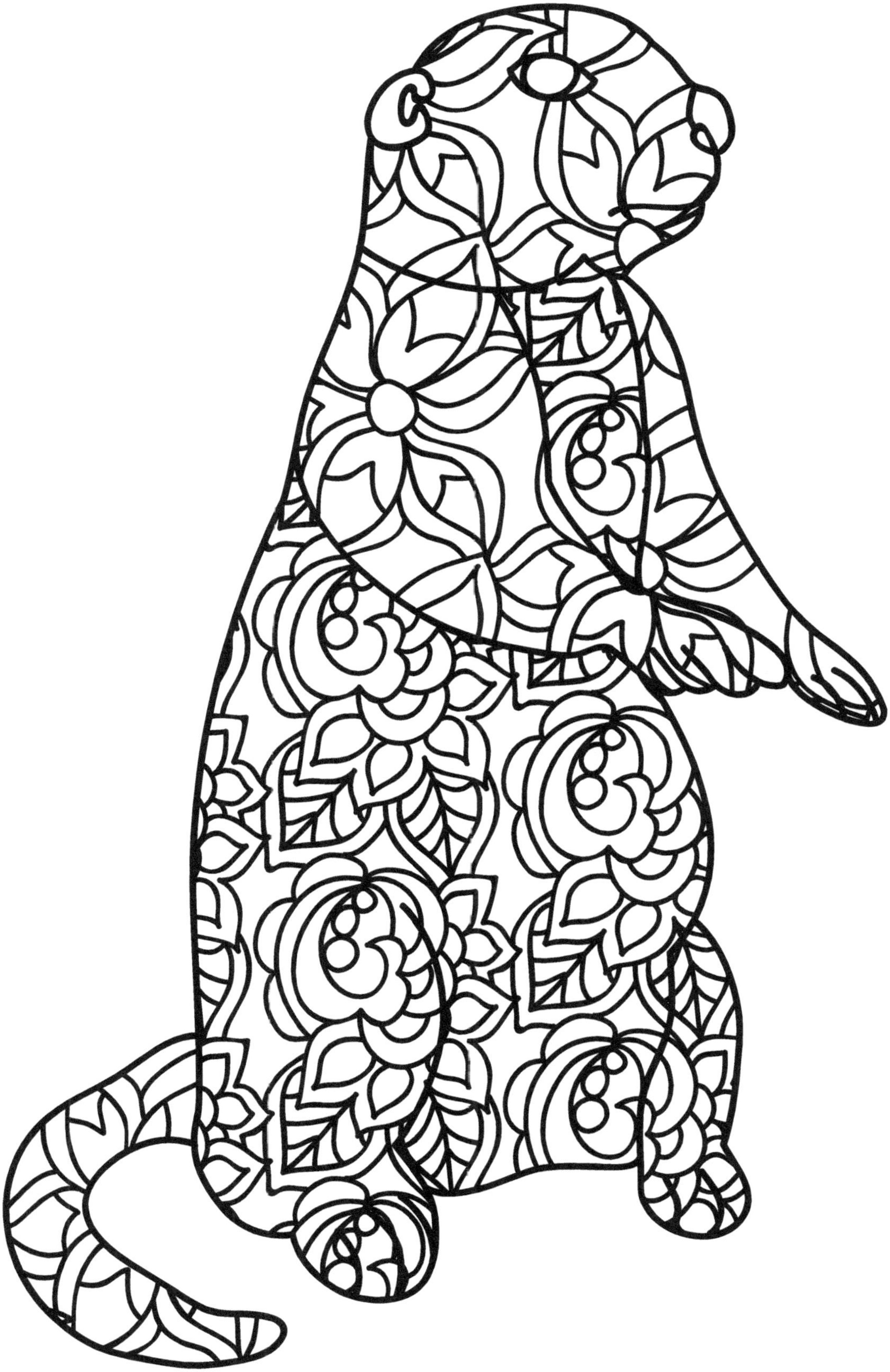

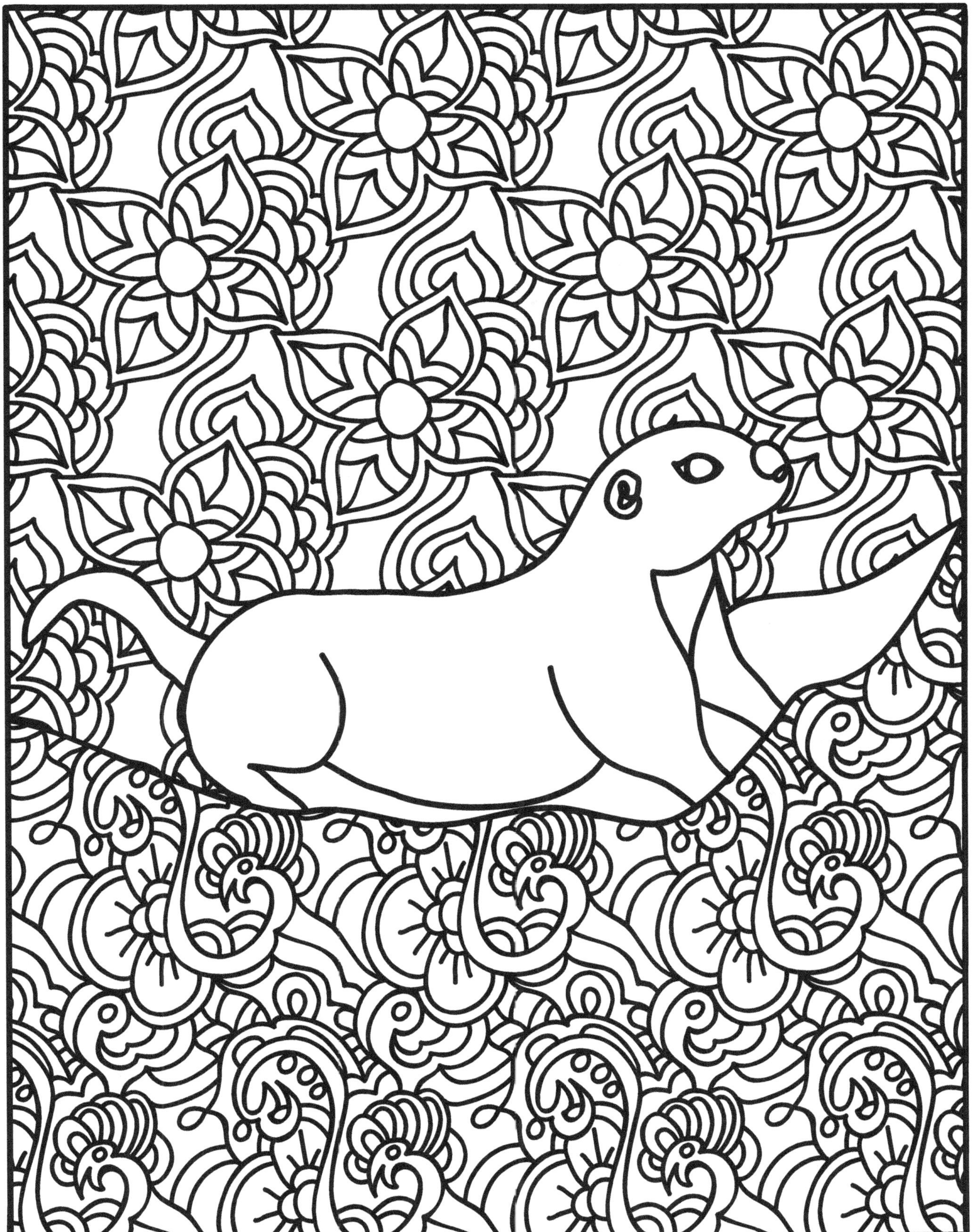

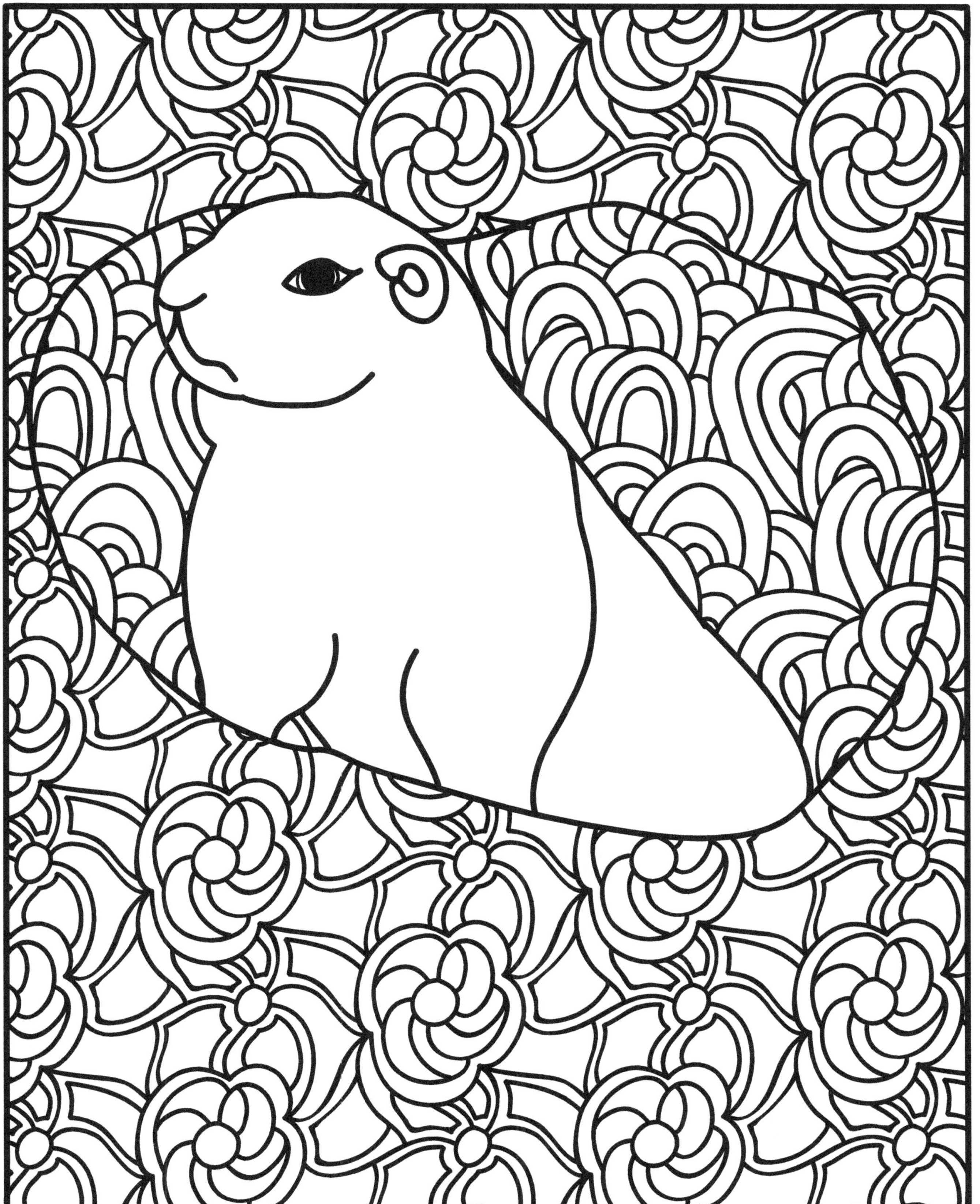

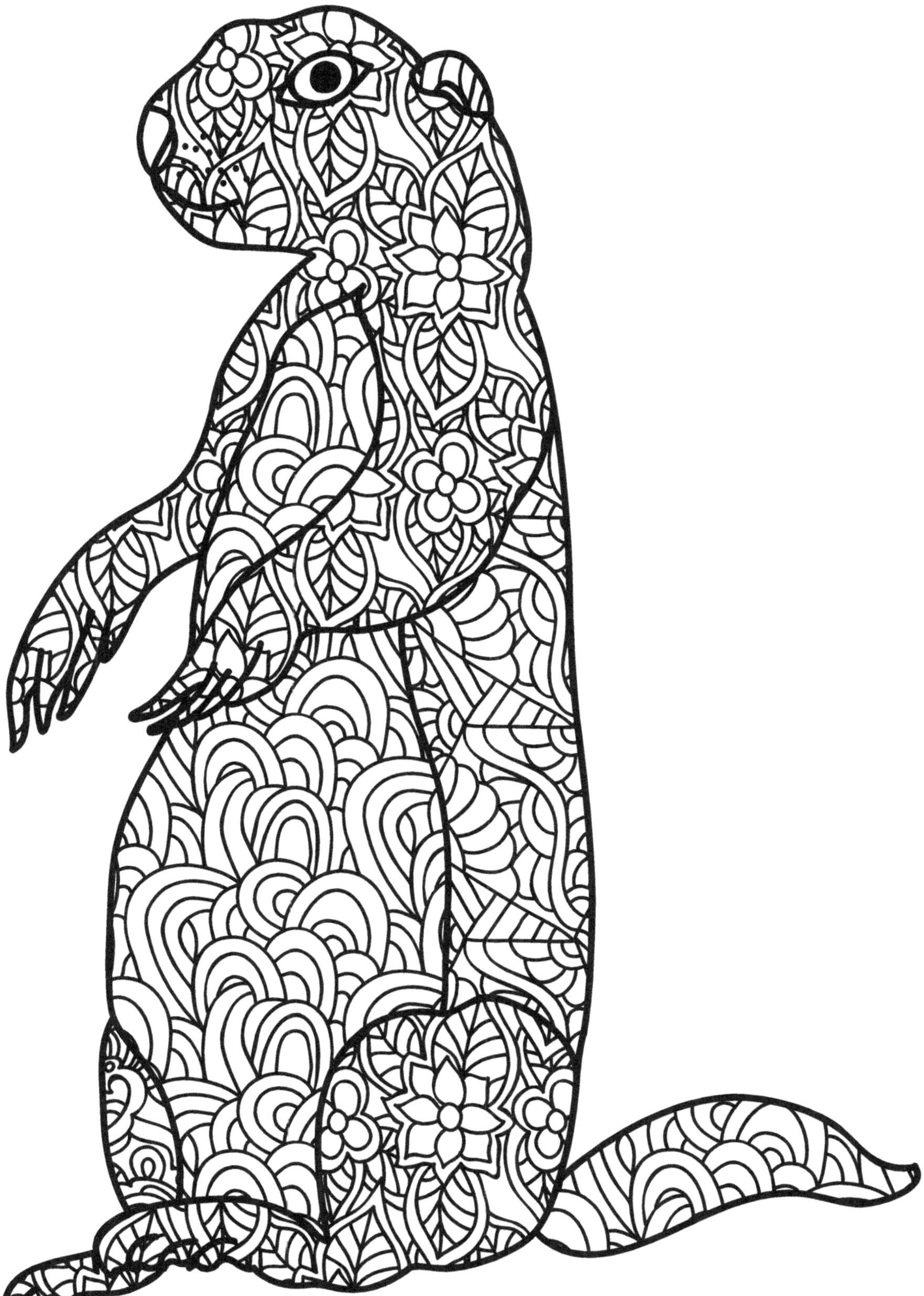

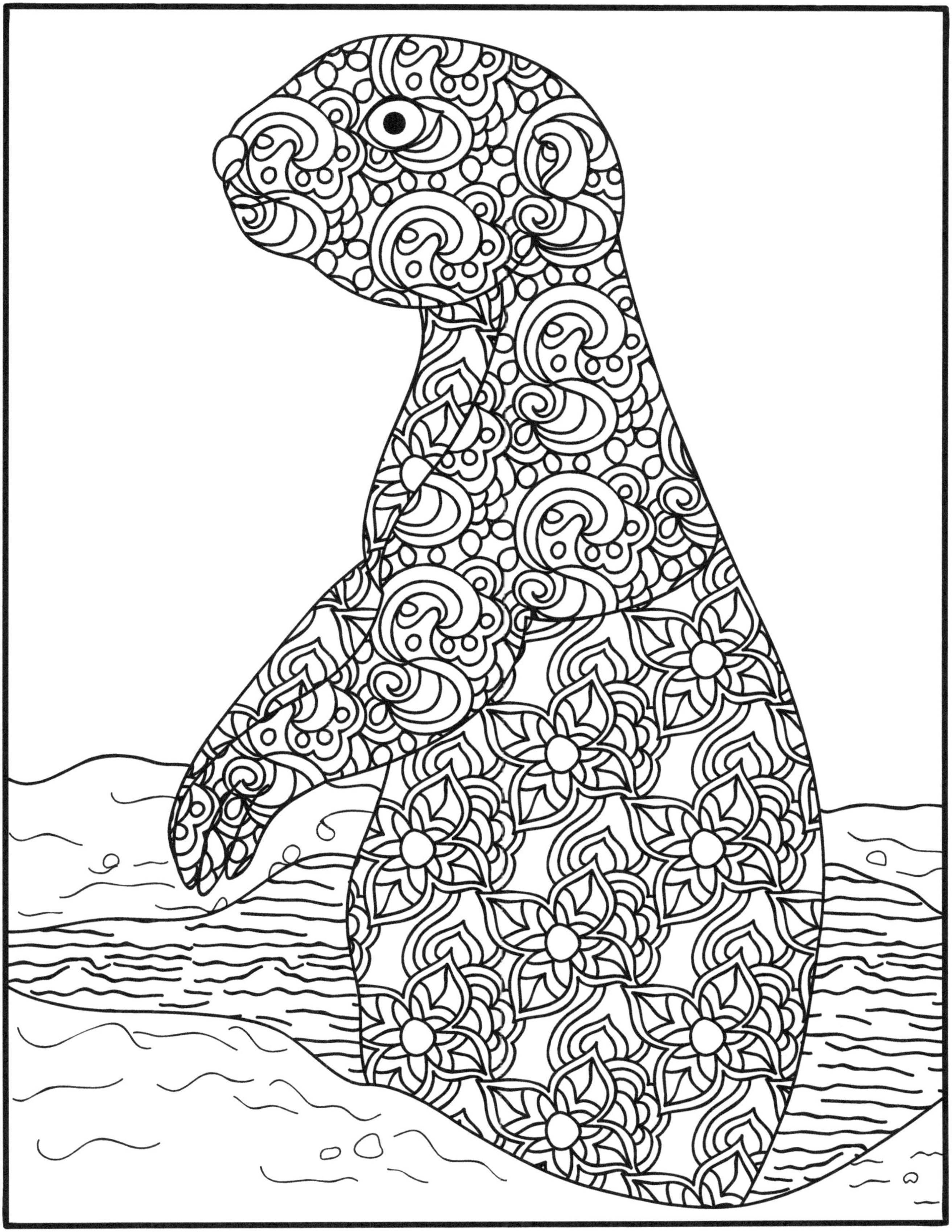

COLOR TEST PAGE

COLOR TEST PAGE

www.ingramcontent.com/pod-product-compliance
Lightning Source LLC
Chambersburg PA
CBHW080621220526
45466CB00010B/3417
* 9 7 8 1 6 7 3 6 7 7 1 3 3 *